# Where

# Will I Be

# Tomorrow?

# Where Will I Be Tomorrow?

## Text and photographs
## WALTER RINDER

CELESTIAL ARTS
Millbrae, California

Copyright © 1976 by Walter Rinder

CELESTIAL ARTS
231 Adrian Road
Millbrae, California 94030

First Printing, September 1976
Made in the United States of America

**Library of Congress Cataloging in Publication Data**

Rinder, Walter.
    Where will I be tomorrow?

    I. Title.
PS3568.I5W47        811'.5'4            76-11360
ISBN:  0-089087-163-9


1 2 3 4 5 6 7 − 81 80 79 78 77 76

# Dedication

To all of you, wherever you may be now, who believed in me and had faith in my motives by allowing your pictures and experiences to become a part of this book.

To my young friend Danny, who once said to me, "I remember you watching, to learn what I didn't know of myself, to help me to grow. I remember how tenderly you touched me, wanting only for me to feel the pleasure and honesty of your love."

To my close friend, Frank Jenkins, who freely shared his world of the South with me (where the seed for this book began to grow), expanding my knowledge and unselfishly giving of himself. "What is extreme today is tomorrow's new frontier." (Frank Jenkins)

A special appreciation to Ruth and Hal Kramer of Celestial Arts who have been constant with their faith in me.

My friends, my lovers, and strangers yet to touch, may this effort contribute to a new awareness within man.

*Walter Rundel*

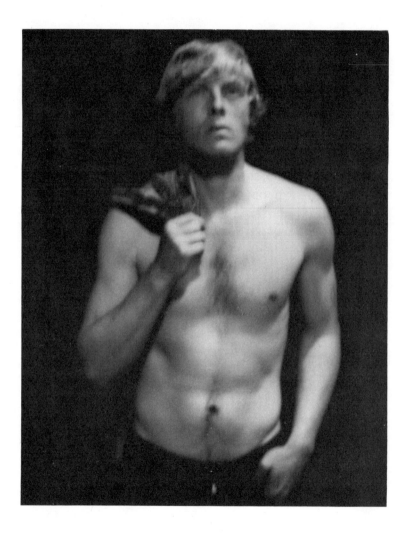

# I

# Being
## Free
# Isn't
## Easy

Being free, isn't easy . . . ask the kid who ran away from home or the kid hitchhiking around the country. Ask the person who quit a steady job working for someone else, if managing his own time to support himself is easy. Ask someone who changed a familiar life style for a new way of life filled with unknowns if it's easy. Speak to the immigrant who left his country for the freedom of another. Ask a person who moved from city comforts to the simplicity of the country. Ask the person who was trapped by social acceptance then chose the freedom of an individual nature. Simply ask a human being who's been in captivity, once freed, if it's easy.

I have never found freedom something we obtained through satisfying just our wants, nor can someone own freedom as a possession. It is not a gift we give when we might feel the need. It is not a way of life we inherit. Only by virtue of our willingness to maintain our perseverance with self-sacrifice and determination, will we achieve any degree of freedom.

My life has been a continuous act of pushing aside obstacles that have been placed in my way to prevent my personal freedom. I have tried to become like the river flowing past the boulders and rocks on its journey in life, not allowing anything to deny its destiny, its movement.

Being free is the most difficult way of life to live. It carries the greatest prospects of loving and fulfillment both for ourselves and our fellow man. Always knowing there is a choice and a decision that can be made, sets the mind ablaze with the fire of hope.

Men's minds are littered with ghettos . . . but the same minds contain the space for universal love and understanding. What has happened to detour vast amounts of freedom to civilization's junkyard?

When will we learn from our past, the lies and deceit we have allowed to flourish and those fearful acts perpetuated by each generation? This can change if we will only face the truth even when it hurts or causes us pain. Why do we torment our fellow man with ignorance when we have wisdom at our disposal?

Why does suffering light the torch of our understanding only too soon to be extinguished repeatedly by our fears? Is the sun so bright that we are blinded, to continually wander off the path of freedom? Why are we prepared to sacrifice ourselves upon the guillotine of patriotism or dogmatic ideas or national interests or to a norm that disgusts us when we are repelled by their obvious lack of goodness or honest justice? Who is the enemy? Is it the freedom of difference we battle, that stimulates our aggression?

Everyone deserves the opportunity to develop their talents, expressions of love and interests in their own unique way, according to their conscience. Mankind is agitating against truth when it tries to convert a human being to other than what he feels good with in living his life as long as his actions are not forced upon others. Only through freedom of choice can a man see his truth. Freedom gives us the experiences we need to discover and grow in our understanding of what loving means. No one owns us. Our body and mind and spirit belong to each of us. We are responsible for our actions and our feelings and having this freedom is not easy. It is the only way to comprehend the action of loving one another and find our place in this world of civilization. It is the only way to find where we belong and what we have to contribute.

Maybe our individual needs are more the same than people realize and many of our major differences are an illusion.

Freedom helps us to find out!

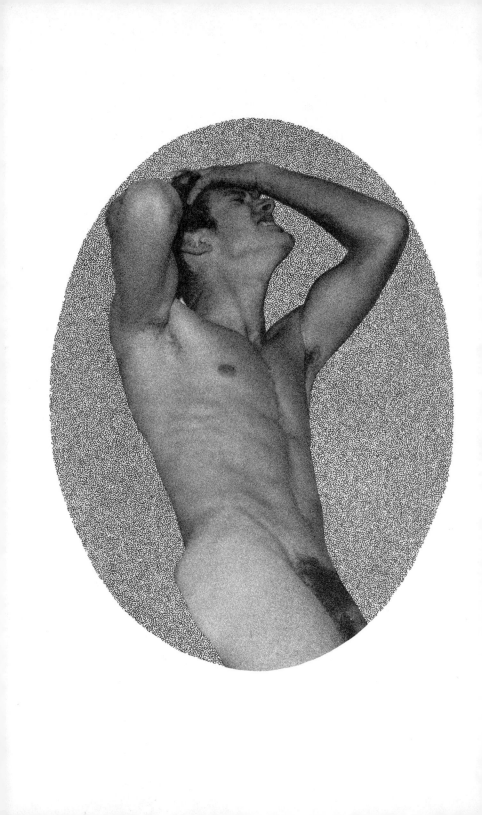

# II

# Conflict

Has man really been created to grow into a regulated life, disciplined to a time schedule, bound by stiff morals, chained to tradition by the acceptance of society? A prostitute paid for by the whims of other men? Did his creator not give him instincts, and spontaneity and sensuality and movement and the ability for an intelligent interpretation of positive and negative? Has this creator of man not foreseen man's divine ability to experience the chaos within his different societies, the harsh realities, the cruel suffering in life, without extinguishing the creative spirit of loving within man's soul? Was not conflict an ever-present part of man's inner growth, man's self-examination of all aspects of his feelings, so he could learn to like himself? Were not all people a part of each man? Were not all cycles of change, on an emotional plane, on a spiritual plane, on a physical plane and on an intellectual plane, a unique and intricate part of his total understanding? Could not pain produce joy of a greater magnitude? From loneliness could there not come a realization of the importance of companionship? Can we know the wealth of love without the poverty in the detachment from love? From boredom could not excitement arise? Cannot opposites complement each other? Couldn't new experiences become as a prophet to us?

When our Creator fashioned nature, in a state of perfection, with opposing forces, with many differences, with a life and death struggle, he fashioned man likewise except for the factors of reasoning and thinking and an explorative nature. Conflicts of ideas, of beliefs, of emotions, of feelings, of justice determined the degree that man could find harmony in himself and in the environment in which he would live.

Conflict is healthy. It serves as a catalyst to improve our capacity for self-realization, for developing our logic, for improving our physical endurance. We must not let our emotions overrule our being in command of our reactions to conflicts. Many people fall to pieces when conflicts arise for they don't seem to see all the positive and negative in any one situation. They greatly limit their minds in exploring all possibilities of the situation, thus, they don't understand why they may feel hurt or have hurt someone else or feel resentful or confused. This makes the conflict turn out to be simply a painful experience, without growth in true understanding.

A tree receives a wound by losing a branch. When the break is healed the nourishment continues to flow throughout the rest of the tree making it stronger. Isn't that also a true part of man? I had a chance to spend some time in Hawaii when I was younger and have many times visited the Big Sur coast when I lived in San Francisco. It seems ironic that many years later the trees would teach me a concept I now want to share. The palm trees in Hawaii appear strong and outwardly very beautiful, their long narrow trunks sweeping toward the sky. On top, a cluster of fan-like leaves rustles when the ocean breezes run across the islands. But, in reality, inside the palm trees are brittle and shallow-rooted. One big storm could knock many of them to the ground.

The cypress trees along the northern California coast are twisted and gnarled and scarred from the

15

pounding of the storms that are numerous in that area. The roots are strong, searching for nutrients that are scarce among the rocks and cliffs that they grow upon. They have weathered the forces of nature which are harsh, becoming strong and beautiful in their own way. I know this is true for us. . . .

The pressures, the hostilities, the stubbornness, the rejections that we encounter and our ability to deal with them will determine the process of our maturing into a strong human being. A person who is strong in fairness, in judgement, in praise, in security, in confidence, and in experiencing their love, is a pillar of loving and an example to others. What a beautiful example, to know a person like this and learn from them.

When we see the bad side of a situation, feeling only negative energy will be the outcome. Or if we see the positive side of a situation feeling only good can come from it I think we lose hold of a truth that could propel our understanding to greater limits. Every act has both positive and negative directions. Every movement can have many interpretations. There are black and white and shades of gray which can create many choices and deductions which are in our power to reason. We should collect as much knowledge as possible to see where the reaction or actions will lead. Our weighing the balance creates intelligent and meaningful decisions. Conflicts can become teachers in our learning about ourselves. An uncluttered mind will feel conflicts as food for growing into healthy, loving beings, who can intimately love both other men and women.

16

# III

# Thoughts Concerning Loving You

*Your Independence*

GET UP YOUNG MAN
DO NOT COWER WITH THE REST
DO NOT SHIELD YOUR HUMAN EMOTIONS
FOR THE WEAPONS OF THEIR WORDS
CANNOT PENETRATE A STRONG RESOLUTION.

STAND UP . . . WITH PRIDE
RENOUNCE THEIR THREATS
AND PROCLAIM YOUR INDEPENDENCE

BECOME A NEW BREED OF MAN

# Why Didn't They Know?

They said you did not adjust to their norm, you were different. These were your parents' words, those of the schools you attended, your society's words. They said you couldn't get along very well with people. You were immature, by their standards, moody and kept your feelings inside.

Together, we discovered, didn't we, that all you needed and wanted was to touch . . . to show affection and be shown affection.

Why didn't they know?

It was so simple!

# To Write of Love

To write of love a man must have plunged into life
having endured the isolated and lovely desert of dejection,
climbed and challenged the mountains of awareness,
roamed the abundant valleys of intimacy,
allowed the winds to move him upon
the seas of his silent longing,
and when he arrives at the homes of men's hearts
his knock should be gentle and his greeting sincere
and when he is bid to enter
his intent should be to fulfill love's needs and
give love's peace
though he may receive love's pain and love's sorrow
for love's purpose is to understand,
love's motive is to stimulate and increase
the expression of the beloved

man, hear with your heart
man, see with your hands
man, touch with your mind
man, feel with your spirit
then, listen to the silence of another
for in that silence they speak to you

embrace loving as it is a kindred spirit
that will never leave you, for all else is not permanent
and, with the passage of time, will vanish

## An Affair with Life

FAIR YOUTH . . . ABLAZE WITH VITALITY
THE FUTURE MAN YET TO UNFOLD
SONGS OF LOVE UPON YOUR LIPS
YOUR FLESH SPARKLING WITH YOUR
HEART'S DESIRES
THE WORLD IS MADE NEW FOR YOU EACH DAY
AS YOU HAVE YOUR AFFAIR WITH LIFE

# A Young Man's Words

only through loving will
you reach me
only through patience will
you teach me
only through kindness can
I hear you
only through trust will
I not fear you
only through honesty can
I believe in you
only through understanding can
I receive from you

## You Ran Away

I once loved you
> for you needed a father

I once loved you
> for you needed a companion

I once loved you
> for you needed a friend

I once loved you
> for you needed adult, male guidance

I once loved you
> when no one else cared

When I loved you as a man in love with you
> you ran away!

# The Universe

Who is on my side when I cry out? Follow me into the universe. Its gigantic but you can't get lost because everywhere there are truths and everywhere mysteries turn into simple understandings. Being lost does not exist, nor does the impossible or absolute or right and wrong. There are no partitions when one journeys into the universal awareness.

Man's taught consciousness severs the body and the soul long before its intended time of separation according to universal truth. During the short time his known body is alive it struggles with partitions so as to confuse his mortal journey.

When you look out the window of your body, is your vision blurred by the twilight of confusion, or can you hold the universe in the palm of your hands, as clear as crystal?

## Please Be Gentle

Every day the young man would throw himself into living. Those days that he met a person, involvement starting anew, and he gave them his heart, he would say silently . . . please be gentle as it has been broken many times and has become very fragile. I have mended it with hope but even hope is not strong enough to assure that it will stay together. Please don't abuse it with your games. Tossing it around will surely cause a weak spot to break open, and, if by chance it is destroyed, then no one else will be able to use it again.

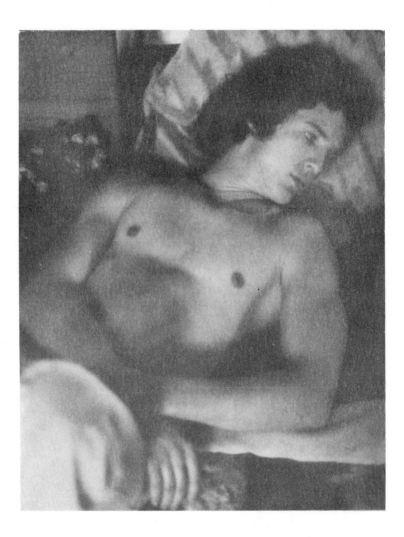

# IV

## Goodbye
## to
## Love

# Goodbye to Love

There was a boy named Danny
who wandered many lanes
you asked him where he came from
too many to recall their names

He'd been to Phoenix city
old Dawson and Timbuctoo
New York and San Francisco
he'd done a thing or two

He'd seen the cities come and go
and still he was alone
for in his search to be himself
he never found a home

Well one black night while others slept
onto the machine he stepped
taking the road to that one fork
where death and oak trees met

His cycle was white and made of iron
his nerves were made of steel
he said, "Why not? Who gives a damn?
I've wounds that are yet to heal"

Fifty miles of open road
as clear as an arrow's path
just Danny, the night and the little machine
and the breath of human wrath

"All you can have of me," he said
"is the dust that lay at your feet
I'm here and I'm gone like the wind that I am
and the dawn that I'll never meet"

From somewhere back in the city of light
a voice cried loud and shrill,
"Danny, come back, come back right now
come back or you never will"

The voice was like the wind in the field
that whizzed right by the seed,
no warning came through the piercing sound
of ignition, machine and speed

"I cannot live in this world," he cried,
"not loving as I feel
for isn't love the reason
that our loneliness is healed"

*Goodbye to Love*

The road was dark, the sky was black
his motor was flaming red
Go ahead, Danny, open her up
You've got to go ahead

He clutched the bars, his body tense
sweat poured down from his brow
for up ahead he saw the spot
it was too late to turn back now

The machine it roared, the rubber whined
like souls await and dying
his speedometer read one hundred and twenty
his mind and heart were crying

He seemed to be going so very fast
he seemed to be standing still
white cycle, white line became but one
both racing in for the kill

Danny, come back, oh please come back
Don't give up your life so soon
We'll go away, just you and I
and talk by the light of the moon

Danny look up at the face of God
look up, look up and see
that truth is what you hold inside
and that can set you free

As dawn breaks through a cloudy sky
can be seen a mass of white steel
shaded by gnarled, grotesque limbs of oak
His red mangled hands no longer could feel

All he's left is the memory of
a young boy's shattered dream
who one dark and windy night
took a ride in his little white machine

"Who you love or how you love
it didn't matter," he said,
"it's only that you love, that's all,
not who's sharing one side of your bed"

But they accused with pointing finger
placing shame upon his love
until he couldn't stand it
so he said goodbye to love
        so he said goodbye to love

# Epilogue

this poem you've read is true, my friend,
the boy of eighteen loved me
his parents, friends and a Christian church
built that road to his destiny

# V

## Dear
## Creator
### of
## All
## Life

Dear Lord:

My people call me Walter Rinder and I am one the multitudes of descendants of human beings you created on the planet Earth. I feel a dire need to let you know I need more understanding, more insight, more wisdom than what seems to have come my way during this time called life.

It's very difficult down here in this mass of what man calls his civilization. I've tried so many ways of living and loving to fit into some harmonious togetherness of my fellow man's acceptance of me and still maintain my individuality—that part of me you created at the time of my birth, a soul unrestricted. My being will not allow my mind to accept many of my fellow man's truths for they shine with injustice. My eyes will not close when my people replace the act of affection and loving with acts of selfishness and the acquiring of material things. The trees of the valleys, the waters of the forest, the flowers of our sacred Earth have touched my sensuality more than many people I've encountered or those who have professed to love me in their limited knowledge of man's taught love. There have been a very few who have escaped to loving without boundaries, and the purity of their love came from you. I've learned more of your truth from the nature of living things than most of man's spoken words or social *doctrines*.

Direct experience from living cannot be substituted. Truth cannot be told us. It has to be lived, using our body as a vehicle as we travel the pilgrimage of our inner self. Why must I suffer so much in the guiding of my understanding? Am I allowed to get tired? Am I allowed a recess from giving? Am I always to be compassionate with people who misuse me?

Always people ask my reason for feeling that the loving of my own sex is as natural, in the building of our lives, as the loving of the opposite sex or loving children, or nature or the arts or in loving you. Maybe my people cannot find the time or the room to love others or a reason to simplify the complicated by just feeling without analyzing that feeling, into rights or wrongs. You always told me that love was the reason and motivation of my actions. You never told me that any kind of loving was immoral, sinful or perverted.

My battling, in the sharing of loving relationships with other males, seems to have become a large part of my existence, my anguish, my struggle to expand this part of me that is held back in its lack of acceptance. This outpouring of energy consumes much hurt and receives even more aloneness. Where do I find the courage to continue spreading loving acts toward everyone even though many are cold to my intentions?

I do not believe that you ever anticipated the male would place so many restraints concerning his feelings toward loving both females and especially other males. Too often I find males cowering under the pressure of what people may say about them when they step from the line of conformity. Many times males hold back in voicing their feelings, let alone act out those feelings of loving me. Lord, I wish to make love rather than spend my life making money!

As long as my society restrains loving of any kind we will always have the need to build prisons, concentration camps, insane asylums, mental hospitals, torture chambers, interrogation rooms and war machines. We will always be afraid to be ourselves and skim over our lives never really knowing the natural highs of living.

My society tries to teach me to live by masculine values and indoctrinates me with what is expected of me to be a socially accepted male. My society censures my intimacy toward other males and nourishes an attitude of the male's dominance over the female. My society tries to scare me with laws and the imprisonment of my spirit to prevent certain expressions of my loving. Lord, I cannot submit to these values or feel compelled to obey those laws that might stop a vital force that is a part of me, that I feel comfortable with. That I feel good with. That I feel is natural to your teachings, "Love your fellow man."

It seems our Christian foundation of behavior desperately needs repairing, revaluation, for it is stained with blood and fear and covered with the bones of our children, of our youth because of the strangulation of loving.

I have acknowledged the need for change but how does one reach my people? Must each of us, in truth, be an example of our feelings, our ideals, our beliefs so others with less courage can grow and gain the confidence that is needed for change? Aren't we vastly more than we appear to be?

The contamination of natural tendencies, mechanical reactions, fear of truth, traditional concepts, particularly stops the male from loving other males. Yet the more times we fall in love the greater is our demonstration in transcending the physical plane of existence toward the spiritual plane, dwelling in your home, of all types of loving. I believe that male's loving other males is much deeper within his heart than he himself accepts. The male's need for affection and an open showing of sensitivity to his sexuality is a tremendous inner struggle. Why can't the male look upon people simply as human beings and show his loving emotionally, sexually, simply, intellectually, romantically, spiritually, according to the depth of his true feelings? Why can't we eliminate the labeling of heterosexual, bisexual, homosexual, gay, straight and just allow the male to be?

When two human beings, any pair of human beings, are expressing love toward each other, what positive energy, what good karma, what divine beauty is spread throughout the world, throughout the universe. When that happens I feel you smiling, I feel your happiness with your creation.

I am saddened by the thought that we may leave our children broken dreams, starvation, frightful thoughts, clutter and fear of their own feelings. Are we to cover their imagination with the umbrella of a mushroom shaped cloud? Will we leave our children our violent acts? Will they claw at each other for acceptance? Or can we leave them a new foundation of loving and understanding so they may build their lives upon the solid rock of your love? Or will they be swallowed by the quicksand of man's conformity?

It is a tragedy for a person to encounter another human being who loves them, when they are not ready to accept their love.

I feel the human race desperately needs to reevaluate its moral direction. Without the nature of all kinds of loving relationships being accepted it is possible that civilized man may decline to a state where he will no longer live to see the glorious dawn of another day of living. How can we, now, become the spearhead for this new growth of awareness? Not carrying a sword but the action of loving each other as we thrust forward. Can we invade the hearts of men and conquer their fear with loving acts?

Lord, am I assuming too much in the words I speak in this letter? Am I a fool's dreamer in believing each person I meet has a vast reservoir of love and goodness, yet to be realized? Is my idealism, my romantic nature not practical or workable among my fellow man? Is my truth only my truth and not my people's?

Please, oh please, give me a greater understanding of how to reach my people, to touch their lives with the hope, the motivation, the strength that we, together, can find a more expansive expression of our loving. Please help me to understand. My soul is yelling to be set free, otherwise my reason and purpose for living can never be certain nor my direction clear.

# VI

# My
Experiences

# The Mall

The mall was filled with afternoon shoppers. In the center was a circular fountain surrounded by cement benches where I sat watching the people living out their everyday lives. I hoped one young man or woman might step out of the parade and take the initiative to say hello and stay awhile, maybe to share what I needed to give. For hours they passed in all directions. Occasionally one would look my way until my eyes met theirs, then, as if afraid of confrontation, looked away to the safety of the shops or tile floor which was much less personal and had not the human touch.

After awhile I began to get bored with their games and my mind began to focus upon my past. One young man in the mall triggered an incident, because of his physical appearance reminding me of someone I shared love with a long time ago. I began to trace that time in my youth when a friend and I sat upon a southern California beach. He had just turned eighteen and was confused in what it meant to be a man according to society's code.

The sea was growing dark and the golden light deepened into the night shadows of the clouds. Creatures of the shore were abundant as the day's heat gave way to the frivolity of a cool wind. The high tide came to erase civilization's marks upon the sand. The surf continued to carry the tales of the sea, to land rovers like us, who could only know vicariously the excitement as the wind-filled sails and the rhythm of oars moved men toward their destinies.

The beach took on a new soft light as the full moon began slowly to move among the stars. My friend was extremely shy by nature, a kind of shyness that was not as apparent to others as it was to me. Surprisingly, as the movement of life surrounded us, he spoke these words and I knew he was on a new threshold in his understanding. "Will there be a time for us? Will today run away like most days have, leaving non-movement as the builders flee from the building? Let's make this night last as long as we choose, gathering all our beginnings into tonight. I want to throw my fears, I want to throw my clothes to the wind and walk naked in mind and body into the water, with you beside me, and along the sound of the waves. Let them guide me to a place of safety where I no longer have to be afraid to be what I feel. Let us stretch time, as a woman preparing wool to be spun into yarn, that we may weave a garment of loving no man can rip apart. In the years I've known you, how much you have wanted to share your love with me. But I was always afraid of what others might think of me. I never wanted to escape from loving you. Deep inside I only wanted to escape to loving you. Tonight my destination has been reached and now let me rest with you upon this sandy shore."

The time needed to build strength and confidence in this new aspect of his feelings was taken away from us by the voices of other people. His uncertainty came too soon in dividing our friendship and weakening his belief in me. So he crowded back into the shell he once had and vowed it had all been a mistake.

# Morning View

I have come back to this place, alone, finding the need to express my feelings upon paper while the experience of early this afternoon is still vivid in my memory. Those happy moments when all of our emotions are centered on a good feeling. When there are no conflicts to interrupt the harmony of a natural high.

My new companion had developed a need to learn my expression of loving, as I needed to learn his. We both had been living in the city for a short time, having lived in places some thousands of miles away. We found it difficult adjusting or accepting the restrictions placed upon the people by the moral fiber of their environment. The social code was extremely strict, the residents adhering to the old traditions which we had already discarded. The awareness of our individuality brought us into each other's lives. We realized we had to hide our growth of intimacy from the piercing eyes of the city streets, from the misguided thoughts of blue uniforms and the legislation that hung over the city like a shroud. We had to cover our motives from the predators who lurked within the boundaries of this mass of humanity lest we become the prey of their vicious attacks or be captured and placed in their human zoo. Fearing exposure we searched for a sanctuary where God's grace would protect his children in the dawn of their love.

As these words begin to describe this day I am now sitting on the edge of what once was a beautiful fountain at the end of a glass enclosed porch. The water rushed from a tube in the wall to a cement pool many feet below which probably held fish and water plants. Leaves and pieces of branches have found their way inside through the many openings that once kept them outside. There is broken glass scattered everywhere, screen doors ripped and splintered laying upon the hexagon red tile floor. The doors were torn away from their purpose. Strips of molding and ornamental facade covered the ground like driftwood washed upon a lonely beach.

Jagged pieces of glass still clung in decorative design where the windows once sheltered the inhabitants from the summer heat and the winter chill. Boards hung from the ceiling, having been displaced from their once neat rows tightly nailed together. Paint and plaster, chipping and peeling from the walls revealed the scars, the nakedness of the wood that now had grown very old and weathered. The giant pillars that surrounded two sides of this structure stood like sentinels, too enormous, too strong to be touched by the pilferage and wanton destruction that man had brought to this once stately Southern plantation mansion. These pillars guard what little is left to remind us of a time when oil lights were ablaze.

The sun now casts shadows of the magnolia trees and the tea olive vines on the walls as it had since the beginning when in the year 1820 a pioneer family chose this spot as their home.

This is only one tiny spot of observation as I sit here listening to the pigeons and mockingbirds flying back and forth to their homes in the rafters. They bring a little life to the sullenness of this fine old lady whose life's struggle was seen by so many only to be forgotten by those she cared for as she lay in ruins, too tired to let her feelings be known.

A bird dog just wandered in from the street, not knowing of my presence. I watch him sniff among the debris with no understanding of the joys and conflicts that once existed upon these grounds, nor the movement of human life that then might have scared him away. Now he felt safe with the stillness.

I got up and walked among the rubble from room to room. Everything of value had been taken. Carved mantels had been ripped from the fireplaces, leaving bricks scattered everywhere. The large sliding doors between the rooms had disappeared. Door handles and light fixtures were all gone. Iron grills were taken, as were the boards and bannister from the main stairway, leaving a skeleton like appearance. Gaping holes were to be found in all the walls. Vandals, who had brought havoc to this mansion, reminded me of the carpetbaggers after the Civil War. They came to strip the South of any wealth or dignity that may have been left after the war had already vanished so much of everyone's lives and the complacency that the agricultural South had been built upon. It wasn't just the issue of slavery that caused the war for the North had industrial slavery of another kind. The real issue seemed to be two different ideologies not being able to live in harmony with each other. Equality of people was greatly imbalanced. Values of money superseded human dignity.

While passing a window the scent of honeysuckle filled me with a delicious feeling reminding me of women dressed in Southern finery. I closed my eyes and my imagination began to form images of these ladies walking with me through the rooms of this house as if I were a guest they were showing around their home. The aroma of the sweet-smelling perfume they wore filled the air with the fragrance of honeysuckle.

I walked up the still sturdy steps to the giant attic where the inspiration for this story began. One beam of light entered through a small part of the roof which had been cut out for a reason I know not. Its height and spaciousness gave me the concept of a giant cathedral but instead of being constructed from the traditional brick or granite it was built of wood left to age naturally, its surface not covered by any material except the elements of nature. Even up there people had maliciously stripped some of the floor boards. I envisioned this room as storing the memories and things people gather, if they are sentimental, reminding them of loves and friends and places that time has a way of erasing. This attic has a special significance for here is where my friend and I, four hours ago, discovered within each other a special feeling. There weren't any barricades built around our hearts, nor restrictions within our minds to cause anxieties to fester in our thoughts. We were free to express the moment. We were not pressured by external forces which outside of this environment might have stopped our participating in the expansion of love. It was our bodies that communicated the silent echo of our longing.

After thirty years of abandonment, left to decay back into the earth, the old lady of Morning View had felt our need and offered herself as a refuge for us to share, with intimacy, feelings that our society would have scorned. Our sharing had also brought a new dimension of life to her silent sadness for once more the lives of people could be heard, the heart's breathing could be felt. The seed of love had been nourished by her spirit. The mansion once more felt the vital moments when man's interaction restored her purpose, her usefulness upon the physical plane of life.

With open arms she embraced my friend and me; our need to share what she had witnessed over the years from the people whose lives unfolded within her hallowed rooms. As we stood upon the attic floor we could feel the vibrations of the antebellum South. The old lady blessed our presence; those who loved her had been too long departed leaving her alone to the greed and havoc of strangers.

Hence, love returned through the two of us, restoring her faith, her diminished hope, her shattered belief in man, and once again she smiled as the proud lady of Morning View.

My companion and I felt that beautiful inner peace when loving takes root in a fertile environment. The decaying of old concepts nourishing the growth of the new was a universal truth we found in the attic of an old Southern mansion in the center of a metropolis on a hot summer's day in June.

# The Magic of Love

We walked through the tall grass to where the white board fence ran parallel to the four-lane highway we had parked near. Another fence of barbed wire attached to the white fence startled us into acknowledging that someone must earnestly want to keep people out or seriously keep something within. We continued to explore the field until we reached a large dead tree which long ago fell to the earth. Sitting down upon the trunk we began one of the richest nights of our lives. It was very dark, except for the billboard sign lit near the highway and the headlights of passing cars as they kept their watch over us.

There were many cows that shared this field with us. Their black silhouettes moved like stalkers of the black hours. Once as we lay in the grass the whole herd ran, as if frightened by something, not too far from us. It was eerie to see their black images in motion.

Among the branches in the tree, which hovered over us like a giant hand, we saw one lonely lightning bug pulsating a tiny light as if it were a star. We both agreed it was the herald of the summer and brought with it a kind of magic we would feel that evening. A few moments later the light from the billboard went out and fewer cars passed on the highway. The hours drew more peaceful as we laid in the grass. Our heads rested on some thistle bushes but we didn't care for the magic made any discomfort that might have occurred disappear. Even the mosquito bites didn't bother us although they found us a delicious meal seldom found in that particular field.

As time passed our feelings begin to transform themselves into another world where love became magic and we became the magicians. Even our words spoke in parables of leprechauns known in our past and rainbows we had walked upon to cross the sky and mystical castles in the clouds our magic could bring down to earth. On starfish we rode across the waves and eagles gave us feathers to sit upon which became our magic carpet. We were not bound to any idea of tradition for each moment was our consciousness and changed as we roamed the entire spectrum of feelings wherever our inclination took us. We traveled in and out of dreams and fantasies. Our vehicle was our free will.

We felt the silver river of companionship flowing through our veins as the waters flowing through the valley of farmers and the growers of the earth. The world we were experiencing was not that of convention but that of the magician. Our stage was the pasture and our imagination unleashed the magic that became as real to us as we believed it to be. It seemed we could become much more than most people, not because we may be successful, wealthy, or intelligent, or even good but because we were free. We knew it. We were being led to the sharing of ourselves few people dare to go for fear of returning back to the common and the ordinary. I never wanted to go back, to what was, if this moment of eternity could only have stayed with me my earthly life. I would have chosen to stay leaving all my material possessions behind for we had it all. The universe was our domain.

I've decided to
become a magician!

## Love Is Now

entering the archway
to a life experience
one early morning
you appeared
dressed in nakedness
of non-pretense
having detoured
from the bustling
arteries
of civilization.
Destiny  proclaimed
our meeting
while I sheltered
under an oak tree
read books of my
fellow poets
to soothe the aching of my body
appease the hunger
of my wondering mind.
When my eyes
first beheld your presence
a comforable beauty

swelled my senses
as nature feels
with the first contact
of spring
as warmth begins
to awaken
the sleeping branches
you glowed
with an aura
radiant and vibrant
whose strength
could bring chaos to its knees
rechannel
the fury of a tyrant's
stormy commands
into gentle phrases
of suggestion.
You a stranger
whose soft confidence
penetrated any
doubt of trust
said by your presence
I am curious
to see what relationship
may develop
with us, two strangers,
whose gift of time
we afford

as a gesture of
friendship
which too often
goes unnoticed
or is taken for granted
by the civilized being.
Hours of conversation
quickly passed
as the day's cycle too rapidly
was approaching yesterday
unfolding personality traits
that mirrored a thousand
inner thoughts
Each moment created
more directness
a more deliberate expression
of feelings
rather than the accepted
generalizations
that people often use
afraid of closeness.
We found speaking truth
was our common ground
although at times
the ground would shake
from conditionings
of the past.
As the hours drew near

for you to continue
your life elsewhere
I felt your reluctance
to leave.
Both of us felt
uncomfortable
at the reality
of separation.
We embraced
not out of courtesy
but our bodies
united
as two lovers
before the time
of departure,
for we had built a bridge
of affection
and began crossing, long
before we parted.
We made promises.
When two people
close the door
on the outside world
of commitments,
responsibilities
of right or wrong,
of good and evil,
totally absorbed

into the now
promises made to keep
if time did not erase
the intent
nor life's perplexities
overshadow
this simple love.
The world we built
was good and comfortable
filled
with meaningful purpose
yet as you left
I felt a sadness
of so many times before
as when feelings
are pulled apart
by emotional strife
by the hidden fear
that binds us
to the condensed safety
of tiny worlds,
knowing
our paths
would never cross again
our promises made
would be dwindled
by the chaos
of a thousand

other thoughts
and questions.
As I now write
with paper and pen
you are already
a yesterday
in my life
as I am with yours,
the substance of our encounter
thinning
with the ingredients of time.
What happens
to the now
when love touches two
then lets go
before the time of building.
If it so be
that right or wrong
truth or fallacy
exists as teachers
dressed as scholars
whose tongue speaks
in absolutes
designating boundaries for loving
then I would choose
the self-knowledge
of my feelings
learning as a free spirit

from experiences
and become an outcast
in the eyes of man
but wise in the
heart of God.
For you,
the one
I made promises to,
showing my truth,
you did forget for a moment
you were a slave
to social thoughts
freeing your soul
to be an individual
while we were together
only again to have
it captured by your mind
when your memory
erased my existence
and you fell back
into the pattern
that was built for you.
I will remember
you tried
to escape.
These words recall
you once touched
my life.

## The Ebbing of Lives

You were seventeen when our lives touched. War and
emotional confusion separated you from me until a
time, five years later, when on a cloudy day your voice,
much more mature, entered my heart as I remem-
bered.

You had again chosen to live with me and become a part of my life. Love seemed to be your reason and you said things I needed to hear, for at that time I knew many people but none special. What had those five years given to you that my loving you had not? Was it your experiencing the war in Vietnam? Was it the death of your parents and brother? The girls you loved, the friends you had, where were they that you came to me alone, leaving your past behind you. After many months we again separated. Is it my love that you run away from or those parts of you that are in discord, churning inside you? We never seemed to have the time to build a foundation. Maybe someday we will for you come back when the need arises, and there is always a chance that in time that need will be strong enough to stand before the truth.

Love is like the wind. We can only see it or feel it when it stirs the leaves and branches.

How many times, more than memory will release, have I felt the saltwater spray upon my face or heard the rubbing together of the cypress branches as the Pacific winds come rushing across the ocean. These cliffs, this rocky shoreline, this sandy beach, I now stand upon seduces that part of me that is alone, once again. I don't fight back anymore. I just allow this rape of my emotions. All the elements of this part of the earth, with their forceful actions, bring me back into the essence of living rather than letting me withdraw into my loneliness.

Our bridge to each other has collapsed, my friend. We can always build a new one. The tools to build are a permanent part of us!

71

## That Night

One night we met and the strangers we were dissolved into a need to spend many hours together.

We tried to communicate our thoughts, I with kindness, you with bitterness, the battle had begun. I listened to your words as they tried to destroy everything I believed in. You tore down my faith with your radical religious convictions. You mutilated peace with your experience in Vietnam. You used your professional musical expression as a weapon to get back at a society you hated. I was a part of that society. Your deceitful love affairs stabbed at your heart as your words came marching forward to do battle. Bits and pieces of your life unfolded in a tone of distrust.

I met your army of bitterness with courage. Everytime your past pushed you down, or began to crush you, or threw spears of guilt or indifference at you, I stood there offering you peace. I sat there looking into your eyes, reaching out to touch you with my love but you struck back and your words began to scream and charge. I met the challenge. Our war of feelings was raging all around us. You again thrust forward with a greater hatred and humiliation of me. Your ridicule lay to ruins every statement I made in a positive tone. In your eyes I was a fool, weak, idealistic, ignorant of the reality of what really was. I reached out to you with words of hope but you said they were only spaces that would keep us apart. I began to feel the weight of your bitterness and fell silent, reaching out to you with both my hands, touching your flesh which was not at war with me as was your mind. Your war subsided, your words made a truce and we made love with our humanness.

The child within you appeared, innocent and playful to love. Peace became the way of our hearts and another part of you was released. You became sensitive, sensual and gentle. Your touch was passionate as if it had always been your way.

Then your past jolted our loving, the truce was suddenly broken and your war of words again fought intently pushing forward, finally becoming the victor. Silently I retreated from the battlefield mortally wounded yet strong enough to heal my wounds and someday to do battle with another embittered mind.

# Circle of Observation

My thoughts were my companion as I lived this day circling the center of my city. When I first awoke this morning, a feeling gripped me to venture downtown and silently watch all the strangers that would capture my attention.

When I arrived I first sat on a brick wall which surrounded a parking lot. For almost an hour I watched people going somewhere, for none stopped except to wait for a traffic light. Most of the faces seemed to be masked in hardness, noninvolvement, tragic survival or fear, but I felt their honest needs shown through their transparent masks. A city full of strangers! A nation full of strangers! A world full of strangers!

My thoughts did make love to some of those faces, this love taking us away from the busy streets of reality to a place where we drank from the dreamer's wine, and the intellect did not substitute for the sharing of love's physical presence. To me those people I saw, who triggered my feelings, seemed to be running away from themselves. They ran hard and fast passing themselves up. In a blur of frantic speed, not being aware, they became entangled in the net of captivity. This day the world of lonely people were passing each other by, only the eyes stayed for a brief moment with a glance of recognition, then darted away as their body continued through the maze of entrapments civilization had established.

Time freezes when thoughts meet on a crowded street, in a restaurant, in a park or a bar where one finds shelter for awhile. If those thoughts would only make sounds, truth could not disguise itself behind the passive flesh.

The secretary, the office worker, the salesperson, the executive, the professional man, the job seeker, and others, dressed in the costumes of life's pageant, afraid to disrobe because of losing their taught social identity. What about their own unique identity?

In a restaurant I saw a human being sitting alone at a table not too far from mine. We exchanged glances, our eyes penetrating the space that often separates the beginning of friendships. Once our eyes touched for many moments, confirming what our minds interpreted. Communicating with our eyes was the only bridge we had built, our bodies could not find a way across. Maybe there was too much debris on the bridge which our past had created and the now could not clear a path. After a time he got up and left looking back at me to acknowledge we were both in the same place with our thoughts . . . one of the many faces I made love to today.

Sometimes I can remember days like today when my fantasy of sharing is more real than my reality. The day has now ended. The night has now captured the city, taking me deeper into the kingdom of longing. More of my footsteps will be found on the pavement before sleep severs this time from living and tomorrow becomes yet another unknown.

The circle has been completed. Ironic how the symbol of love to man has been the circle!

# The Mill

Only with loving actions can you reach me for all other reasons are objectionable and will, with the passage of time, push me out of your life. This is not necessarily my choice but by my nature I begin to drift until the current of loving catches me with its motion somewhere else.

Go home, my friend, and contemplate as you will the unknowns and differences I have shared with you. Deal with my spoken words that a few may have penetrated the confinement of your mind. Your acceptance or rejection of me is of little concern for by the freedom of my spirit in allowing you to know of me I chance being a threat to the security of your limited experiences. Examine the affection I offer without boundaries, within the scope that your learning allows. I have hoped to increase your awareness by my being a new experience for you and have held your hand with understanding knowing you may be frightened by the truth that often wears the monstrous mask of fear.

Go home, my friend, and if you have chosen confusion seek my counsel again that we may continue to grow. Or if your choice be that of not relating to me then I will walk the other way, never again to be a bother or burden to your fireside complacency. If you wish to share the me, that you discover is within you, then we can unite two loving spirits upon the plane of the physical. If you wish to understand this difference you feel is between us then let us discover, not tolerance, not acceptance, but the realization that we are much the same in feelings and needs and much of that difference was only an illusion.

# A Stranger No More

From the absence of light, your sensitive face illuminated my tired spirit. For the day had been long and the miles many since the early hours of the morning waved goodbye as I started on my journey's way. Five hundred miles from home brought me to your town, to rest the night, where fate commanded our meeting.

I could feel your apprehension for the time we would have together was very short, yet the need to share pushed away your indecision that there may never be another time for us.

We found a shelter from the damp, cold night, closing the door on the outside world which was alien to our feelings. Your touch was slow and cautious, yet deliberate, not wanting to miss any part of the body that might give you the knowledge, the security, the comfortable feeling of the human being who had just entered your life. Maybe, you felt, I could fill that portion of love, of need, that only a man could manifest, as you honored and loved your wife for she filled those feelings reserved only for a woman. This male longing, once familiar to you, reached into your mind as you remembered another time, another place, where this expression of love had been your home, but too soon you were sent away, a child of the streets once more, a minstrel of sad songs.

We took the chance in nourishing each other's minds, mindful the words had to be well chosen for time was our barrier and those words remembered might carry a reason to come together once more. The whole encounter happened so fast that as I sit now writing this, already there are gaps in my remembering.

Your touch is what I am feeling the deepest, for it lingers upon my body like the morning dew upon the lawn of clover. Your hands spoke the sounds that echoed in the caverns of your thoughts.

Your lips I felt were desperate in their search for a quiet place to rest where they could linger without the pressure of our social order, wishing time would vanish within a world where caring had no points of departure.

We made love while the fleeting moments teased our longing. There were so many feelings to explore while reality confined us like giant snowpacked mountains to the valley below until spring's thaw would release us to continue our journey.

I wish you were sleeping here beside me for I do not want to touch you with only a memory. Too often in my life have I shared my bed with no one, my fantasy recalling a yesterday.

I know I'll be back for we have left much undone and where there is even a small chance of continued growth I cannot leave the beginning unattended.

Is there room for me in your life? Was the time shared still in your heart as you now are back with your wife and in the security of your home? Questions I cannot answer!

I am happy to have shared the moment, expecting nothing more, for all the moments I have lived are my life.

I lay alone, listening to the cries of the bay, as the foghorns wail the sounds of the sea, the boats sheltered for the night until the ocean again beckons their return, as I do yours.

# VII

## The
## Courage
## to
## Love

# The Courage to Love

The Pacific Ocean became extremely restless, churning and twisting as the storm from the Gulf of Alaska poured its fury into the waters tumbling toward the shoreline. The hands of the wind whipped the waves so hard they leaped skyward, until their strength gave out, lashing wildly at the rocks who stood defiantly in their way. These waves, with hoods of white foam, finally subsided, sliding, then sinking, into the grains of sand which were to become their final resting place. This part of the world had seen many such storms as this which, in sculpturing the coastline, has created one of the most beautiful landscapes on the western part of the United States. Dark and light clouds and various shades of gray turned as a giant movie screen. The images of eternity and of the present moved silently across the heavens, speaking feelings of a divine nature.

The young man had traveled three thousand miles to this place of mountains, rain-filled clouds, and this rock and crag shoreline. He had taken the chance and the risk to venture these miles away from his secure world to a different world in which his learning love was felt from a man rather than his accustomed relationships with women. Confusion filled his heart as he had always separated the projection of his feelings into his friendships with males and females in different ways. At this time of his life he began to feel a need to understand more about this feeling man calls love, and this trip was the real beginning of his sacrificing what he was and had been for the man he hoped he could become. His friend had given him the opportunity in experiencing new avenues of communication. Even as he left on this trip his emotions were insecure and his mind uncertain as the earthquake of awareness upset his complacency. Even as the salted spray now slapped against his face this new world had become exciting and also frightening. As he now descended into the influence of his friend's world he began to slowly understand some of his friend's beliefs and his friend's words held more meaning. Their simplicity stood out from the clutter of social dogma. His past began to dissolve as the present became his reality. A reality he knew he had to deal with. This beach, where sights and sounds began to captivate his feelings, revealed to him he was a lonely traveler, far from home yet maybe home was something you carry inside you. Maybe home was where people loved one another.

How incredible he thought, this part of the earth. Too beautiful to be real, but it was real. It was real! With a swift turn he glanced everywhere trying to understand a balance, a continuity between the gentle soft sand, the ferocious water, the monoliths of rocks, the ever changing clouds, the invisible wind, the high cliffs and the creatures of the shoreline who seemed mysteriously to bring everything together.

His friend sat at the base of the cliff, watching him as he discovered a small part of the whole as one would look at a tiny rock which had broken off the face of the cliff. He would feel his friend's eyes following him as he moved in exploring the many facets of nature that stimulated his curiosity or touched his sense of wonder. Each new discovery brought him closer in his contemplation of who and what his friend was. A deeper meaning to their relationship would be brought about by each tomorrow for change was the path his mind followed.

It had been nine months since the thought had first entered his mind of leaving the world of his childhood and his youth. It was at the same time he met his new friend. He remembered it was his friend who had first implanted the idea of his changing his way of life, his attitudes. A life he had become stagnated in yet accepting it as so many people are trapped—without question. Without ever asking themselves is there a better way? Is there more of me to learn about, to experience? Have I really ever loved or been loved? Until his friend came into his life these and many more questions had never been asked of him. He accepted his very conventional way of life as his pattern, even his destiny.

No one had told him he was much more than he appeared to be until he met this stranger in a bookstore one day while browsing, waiting for his girl to get off work. This man he met was quite different than anyone he had ever encountered. Not because of his physical appearance, though he was quite handsome, but his gentleness revealing a wisdom in his eyes, his strong and self-confident manner as he initiated the first hello, "I'm a stranger to your town and would be pleased if you would share coffee with me and tell me of yourself and your city." It wasn't so much the words the man spoke that he felt secure with but it was the sincerity in his voice that he trusted and the feeling of wanting to know about this stranger. To the man's invitation he surprised himself by answering "yes," the word flowed from his lips even before his mind had a chance to think about the question.

This was very unlike him for his tiny world had little room for difference or deviation from familiar experiences or programmed responses. Besides he had nothing else to do while he was waiting for his girl and it wouldn't hurt to spend a little time in conversation, never realizing that this would someday lead to his now standing here at the Pacific Ocean. My God, he thought I'm here. I'm here, visiting this man who only nine months ago smiled and said hello. Now he's my friend and I am finding a special quality, a uniqueness in his ability in exercising his interpretation of love. With these thoughts he turned and looked back at his friend, sitting beneath the cliff, waving his hand in a gesture of companionship. Many of his feelings were still uncertain yet the man's kindness kept penetrating his past beliefs.

The storm began to build and the rain came a little harder. He tightened his jacket around his neck and pulled the hood over his head continuing his journey of self-discovery which he felt at this point nothing could interrupt. The sea gulls over head seemed to be watching him. He'd give them a shy smile letting them know he was thankful to share this place with them, on this day.

Everywhere he walked he felt the vitality of life. Remembering his friend's words, "Collect feelings rather than things," he opened himself to observing all that surrounded this world that he and his friend were spending the day in. He had been collecting feelings since he arrived at his friend's house in the mountains two weeks ago. The talks by the fireplace, the walks in the woods, the beautifully prepared meals, the sharing of photography and old things his friend had collected

in his home. The library of books whose knowledge and insight were a treasure to his limited experiences. Ski trails and snow-laden slopes and a river whose motion stimulated his wanting to explore. Awaking to the sounds of the rapids and the aroma of fresh perked coffee and a warm smile. Affection and tenderness he had never known. A sharing that he once would have shied away from, now seemed natural and no longer alien to his nature.

This man had lived many more years than he had, as he was just entering into manhood. Their separation after their first encounter had given him the many months needed to build the courage to experience more of the man and his world. Yet even now his courage was limited to his leaving his secure way of life and to receiving a part of the man's giving. His new awareness of love was no longer confined to one type of loving intimately, but this feeling was still in his thinking not in his actions. He had much more to learn. His courage was still weakened by his past upbringing.

The rain increased and the clouds grew darker and he and his friend walked back along the tide's edge toward the truck. He put his arm around the man's shoulder, not just for a moment, but kept it there trying to say what his heart could not say or fully understand. He felt comfortable with this moment. As the elements of the sea and the sky and the earth pushed he and his friend closer together for warmth he felt his heart would find, in time, the courage to love.

# Susie and I

Five life-filled years our lives have brought us together and separated us, like the ebbing of the tide, that we may learn and expand to come together and separate and come together again.

She feels comfortable with my nature and loves all those parts of me that others might have misunderstood.

Our loving each other seeks its own aspiration as it is made known to us. Susie does not dwell in the conventional nor let social distractions lead her astray from her seeking the pure knowledge of her soul and mine.

Susie is not satisfied with what is but what can be. Her personal appearance in my life is always filled with the act of sharing love.

I recall a time when she was a part of my art gallery in Portland. She worked as a sales person and was the ambassador of friendship and warmth, greeting those who entered. Many males were uncomfortable with her openness of affection when they came into the gallery. Susie and I on many occasions discussed with others the need to show a more open expression of affection. We were a beautiful balance in communicating this toward both males and females.

How I wish her lessons would mirror the hearts of males for then they would not say of me, "I can only love him mentally but not physically. I can touch him with my mind but not my body. We can communicate with the spoken word but not with affection."

She once said that each body was in apprenticeship to the prophet of loving.

90

# Within You and I

My potential friend, allow me to share my eyes if you are blind. Allow me to share my touch if you cannot feel the beauty that is you. Allow me to share my ears if you are deaf to good thoughts. Allow me to share my intellect if you consider yourself ignorant. Allow me to share my self-worth if you have been taught none. Allow me to share friendship that you may feel your emptiness, finding a need for companionship.

In time you will begin to feel the good and the beautiful. In time you will know the sensitivity of the flesh and a new world abundant with vitality. In time you will hear the voices of loving and kindness upon my breath. In time you will learn of your own intelligence and your mind will be ablaze with new thoughts and ideas. In time you will begin to like yourself. In time your new found love will fill the emptiness of others that were once like you.

My potential friend, all we need is time together. This is the most precious gift you can give to me, as I with you.

You cannot discard your past for it has made you what you are today or what you think you are. Neither can you use your past as a crutch to lean on. Your wounds will mend soon, for I will tend to them. Nor can you continue to use your past to become embittered or not care because then you suppress your growth toward preparing for your future.

Neither can the absence of love's teaching be your criteria for wasting away another day of waiting, of feeling sorry for yourself. What has eluded you was the realization that your past was a school and you have yet to experience much knowledge the cycles of change will bring.

So your past be as it may, you will continue to learn. Try and be tolerant and patient of the way your past has taught you. Become aware of your present and the opportunities that are given to you.

I am now sitting in the coffee shop wondering if you have the courage, will take the chance and come back to meet me as planned so we can spend several days together at my mountain home, so I may share a new environment with you, new experiences that you may find are a part of you. As the hands of the clock move slowly toward the designated hour my hoping grows more intense and with each person that walks through the entrance of the coffee shop my anticipation jumps within the pit of my stomach, hoping it to be you. Many different faces come in but only your face can quiet my silent desperation. I keep glancing up at the clock and watching the front entrance for I have nothing else to do but wait and write about my waiting. Right now my life revolves around you for that was my commitment and my promise. I do feel nervous because I care. My love does that to me.

Please don't run away from the present because of your past. Come in from the city streets. Come in from your father's scorn and your mother's not loving you. Come in from the deceit of your world. Come in from people who seduce your body for their own pleasures and lustful purpose, not being concerned with the soul that lies within that body.

My potential friend, I care
about you but will you give me the
opportunity to show it!

# My Friend and I

My friend and I spent the day together, just the two of us, for we needed no one else, exploring each other's feelings of our many yesterdays, of now, of future times, both struggling in the hope of finding love in a torn and tattered world.

He took me to the wooded countryside where he grew up, driving slowly along the winding road, the trees reaching toward the sky like spires of a great citadel, the bright green moss, the white birch bark, the yellow leafed plants, the brown decayed logs blending together like large stained glass windows. We drove up to the home he and his dad had built. It was on the top of a hill overlooking a coastal valley where the river made its way slowly toward the sea. All the while he told me of incidents of his youth, both of us laughing at his wildness and the carefree things you do when you're young.

We arrived at a little town, where he spent his years as a kid, just a short distance from the coast. He began reminiscing as we drove by the old high school telling me with pride of the moments when he played football and basketball, honoring his school. Then we came upon the wooden house where he lived, painted yellow now, the picket fence gone but the memories were still there. We stopped at a restaurant in his hometown, talking to some old folks who remembered. I listened to him asking about some of the kids he used to know and my mind wandered to my younger days thinking about the friends I grew up with and the things I felt. We were both from such different environments, if we had met then we wouldn't have realized friendship. The years of our youth that then would have separated us now are bringing us together for we both have come to understand the importance of experiences where values change and feelings are set free.

We drove to his parent's dairy where I met his mother, father and brother. I stood by the window looking out at the grazing lands of their farm and the tree-covered hills holding back the fog, remembering my boyhood home when I looked out the front yard at the avocado, walnut and tangerine trees surrounded by a large green lawn, all this within a large city.

We left his home traveling through the mountains. At the summit it began to snow. It was beautiful and I wished we could have stayed there instead of going back to the city. I thought of a day like this ten years ago when another friend and I drove through the mountains near Flagstaff, Arizona. It snowed then, as now, and I loved him then as I love my friend now. I haven't heard from or seen that young man for years. How can human beings who were so close drift apart so abruptly?

The next thing I realized, we were out of the mountains on a freeway headed toward the distant light of the city. I looked over at my friend, wondering how to stop this drifting of human souls, who once touch with love then sprint away as if in a race with life. But where is the finish line? Who wins?

# Afraid of Being Afraid

He was kind, considerate and cared about things. The type of young man parents hope their son grows up to be. The kind of non-rebellious citizen the ruling class hopes for. Giving four years of his youth to military obligation, working eight hours a day, supporting his own apartment and contributing to the materialistic economy. He typified the good character of the average young American male. Now this is what he appeared to be in the eyes of other average Americans, males and females.

He and I met, by chance, in a craft shop as he happened to be looking at a display of my books. After a few minutes of conversation I realized immediately he wasn't average but quite a unique loving spirit wanting to unfold as the man he thought he might be, not what others had made of him. Nobody in his life had yet come along and recognized this beautiful creature of humankind so he outwardly became what was expected of him as he grew up in the tube of conformity.

He triggered my perception of his true nature simply by the energy of his caring. As we grew in our friendship I could not help but continually reveal my feelings toward his special soul. It was crying to be let out of his beautiful physical form. I hoped I could become a mirror so he could see a living example of those parts he felt the deepest need to outwardly

project. He wanted to change his average life to a new level of fulfillment. I hoped we would journey together into the valley of enlightenment where his natural talents, his compassion for his fellow man, and his charity could be homesteaded in the soil of civilization.

The last thing I said to him before we parted was, "Can you sacrifice what you are now for what you can become? Can we share loving?" He said he was scared. I said scared of what. He said he was afraid of being scared.

# The Fireplace in Your Heart

I didn't want to go, to leave you. I wanted to stay with you forever but I don't know forever. I wanted to fulfill the needs that only my being could but time clawed and tore at my mind pulling me away. I wanted to give to you the world, but the world was not mine to give.

As I drove away, a hostile world faced me once again but I knew I was stronger.

I stopped the truck at the end of your valley, by the old bridge and stood upon a part of you and my tears fell upon the earth to mix with the rain and the patch of snow beneath my feet and I kissed a tree and the tears came faster and I yelled for my creator to give me the wisdom I lacked and the knowledge that has eluded me and to stop the testing of my soul in seeking truth. I could not stop the crying and I didn't care because my soul was being released and I felt fear that it was not enough.

Every few miles I stopped the truck to write my

feelings so they would not escape the world unknown, for you needed to know, more than just the river and the tree and the mountains. They have witnessed my flights from suppression all the years of my life.

As the miles began to separate us further, my contentment mixed with uncertainty, my having received fused with my longing, my reality challenged my dreams and fantasies. For you touched my nakedness with the warming rays of pure love.

Goodbyes are like the universe that I can't comprehend. In this man-made tradition of goodbye I am uncomfortable and would rather sneak off in the night, unnoticed.

I just saw a young man in a wheelchair as I drove by an old shack and he appeared not to have any legs. He smiled and waved since I was going slow and I looked at him. I wanted to smile back. I wanted to stop and give of myself, a hug, a kiss an expression of my concern. Maybe a few words of understanding. Maybe he needed me to make love to him, for time controlled me like a master. I its slave. He will never have known me or I him. How often in life we pass love or its projection because of time involvement with things.

Your world will not let me go, for your truth is stronger than you realize or have ever known. You had expectations before I came but you were flexible in reevaluating who I really was, and who you were. You took the chance, the risk to reveal some of your personal feelings. You opened your safe world to conflicts, to pain. I, as an individual, uprooted the complacency you had built, my motive only being I cared enough to be myself.

It is not enough to be what we are, or think we

are, for life reflects we are so much more. Each of us has an awareness that our capacity is greater than what we appear to be to ourselves and to others. Therefore penetrate the shell of flesh and bones, for within lives a soul too beautiful for words, too magnificent for thoughts, too eternal for comprehension, too filled with love for conditions. A soul simply wishing to manifest itself into life by feelings, to be understood and to understand.

We spent a greater part of four days with the intellect, a beginning. Now let us build also with our sensuality.

In the giving of yourself by loving other people, you have to lose forever a part of yourself and that's the least that happens. In pure love, you think not of yourself, you step out of I and give spontaneously from your heart. It is triggered by the other person's needs and maybe their lack of awareness of themself. If you know your energy is endless then the giving is constantly being replaced by new energy which regenerates itself. The actions of love rejuvenate love. Can people become so secure with themselves that they do not look for false motives, nor are they threatened by the intentions of others? Can they not fear sharing love's aura or become afraid of change? Can we, with others, build this type of world on your land and become an example to the world of civilization? Where does devotion and commitment and responsibility play a part in our feelings?

I have dedicated my life to awakening other people to loving each other, to care and to feel and propagate this emotion as a way of life. I have no insight or perception without love.

Soon I will return, for destiny demands that we build a deeper awareness of our intentions and reasons. They must not be selfish for we must care for each other as we care about ourselves, and open our hearts and our understanding to other different types of people to be a part of us as long as all our goals are the same, revolving around loving. Difference is beautiful when it is built on the solid rock of understanding. Can pride give way to humility that is receptive to concepts and ideas that are different, that is the balance? That no one person has all the answers, no one is more important than another except where our individual talents are projected? Where there are unselfish actions, emotional competition does not exist.

You must reveal, within your heart, what I can fulfill in each of you that love or life has not, and make it known that I can read the scrolls of truth that our creator wrote for man. What can I contribute to our ideas? A new way of life that could fulfill the dreams that we all may have, that you could not have without me.

I must search within myself: Can I come into your world, the foundation already formed by your sweat and toil, the beginning a yesterday? Can I fulfill my needs by being a builder or do I need to pioneer my own world, laying my own foundation, scratching the dirt and pushing aside the rocks to plant the seed that is me? Could I continue to scratch the dirt and push aside the rocks for other seeds that are carried by the winds of belonging to me or do I, with that special person (lover), scratch the dirt and push aside the rocks to plant our seeds, then share with others in the building?

104

In time the way
will be made known
to me

## Give More Than You Take

I have seen him many
times touching life and
each time he gave
more than he took.

# Memo

I met a man at a gas station while they were filling my tank, so I could leave early in the morning for the Florida beaches. He had noticed my Oregon license plates and spoke of the great distance I was from home. We spoke of simple things and in the course of the conversation I told him I was an author. There was silence for a few moments then he said, "I've got a story to tell," then looked at the ground, his head bent as if the weight of his thoughts could not sustain his composure. I patiently waited for him to reveal the story but he continued with the ordinary words one says upon meeting a stranger. I repeatedly asked him about his story. His face would stiffen then relax as he asked me about myself not hearing my question. He was a very common looking man with no noticeable outstanding features but I sensed there was more to him than the obvious. Life has taught me to look beyond the common and the ordinary, for inside each human being is a story, exiled from the social norm, astray from the sanctuary of acceptance. We continued talking and again I asked him about his story. Reluctantly his words became audible, from a whisper he began to speak in a sharp, deliberate tone. "For two years I was in a concentration camp during World War II." He stopped abruptly, looked around, then his eyes met mine, "and I saw babies tossed into the furnace, children ripped from their parents' arms never to be seen again. The sounds of the living knowing they were going to die, their minds tortured by that thought. Yes, young man, I've got a story."

My gas tank being full I said goodbye to the man, paid my bill and drove off into the sun. Only after I was many blocks away did the meaning of what the man said hit me. I quickly turned around and headed back to the station but of course he was gone. He had wanted someone to write his story, for he didn't know how. Maybe I could have if my mind hadn't been detoured with thoughts of the beach and the friends I was to meet that evening. What meaningless jargon filled my mind. What stupidity erupted in my feelings that I didn't take the time to spend with this human being who was reaching out to me. He wanted the world to know he was one of the few survivors of mankind's extermination programs. And I was caught up, as most people are, with their complacent thoughts and patterns of living and mechanical reactions so as to let slip by me a new experience that could have added greatly to my understanding.

I am now reminded of the story I once heard of the frog and the boiling water. If you put a live frog in cold water and slowly turn up the heat under the pan he will die without knowing what is happening. But if you put the same frog in boiling water he will immediately jump out of the pan. So it is with the human being when freedom and justice is slowly taken away from him.

I realized this man had been one of the signposts to my destiny though I was blind to understanding. "Oh what fools we mortals be when enlightenment serves us in our hunger, the morsels of experiences."

As I write this in a restaurant I'm looking over at a family, mother, father and two young teenage sons, eating at the table across from mine, and I see one of the young boys naked, covered with blood his flesh ripped open, already the maggots are at work lying on the ground, a swirl of dust covering his mutilated body as the tanks roared on toward the horizon and I cried because I felt helpless, except in writing you this memo.

# He Must Find a Place

He went home . . . to where he called home. The place of solitude of quiet reckoning, to conceive who he was, what he was, so he would be able to navigate his own personality.

He thought, "There is no issue stronger than myself. There is no tissue greater than my flesh to construct love with. Shame on me for converting my life into fearful responses, into weapons that annihilate human love, that decay human goodness. That turns me into a crippled animal returning from the battle that rages in my heart."

He looked at himself and saw with clear-eyed vision what he had inflicted upon the lives of others. He looked into the mirror of his deeds and saw where promises, caring about others, compassion, bled from the hurts he caused by his scarred mind.

He cried out, "We are all on trial as we have put truth on trial. I, as a part of the jury, prejudge other men for their loving me because I was taught it was wrong. When this love is given to me I run in disgust for I am a coward, afraid to understand. I convict them with my words and send them to their grave by deserting them when they reach out to touch. What salvation can I feel in my bitterness. Can I count the many times when my verdict, my condemnation crippled the love within another male? Can I count the many times when my lack of responding to their affection wounded the confidence loving had given to another male, and all the carbon copies of me sheltered me from this loving friendship, because they fortified my ignorance? Can my sheltered attitude continue to rebuke the honesty of this love simply because I fear it may be a part of me?"

"I MUST FIND A PLACE WHERE I DO NOT HAVE TO PARTITION MY HEART!"

# Dune, A Young Lover

*Dune, A Young Lover*

Dune came running through the
branch laden waters
his genitals not imprisoned by cloth,
his taut muscles reflecting
the powerful energy within,
splashing a million droplets
churning and darting in all directions
in his celestial pilgrimage
of search and probe into
the essence of his being.
Taking deep breaths of life
he challenged the
rock's sharp crust
in a blur of speed
past nature's stillness
his restlessness too real
in its understanding
within the complexity
of his people.
His deliverance,
an all encompassing desire
to speed the momentum of his longing
upon the lips of all his lovers
leaping into the flesh
of his creator's divine creation.
Run far, Dune, run fast,
run far, far away

from the entrails of cities
filled with decay
toward your solution
a new birth on this, your
triumphant day.
The river enchances the prospects
of your fulfillment as your heart cries out
"World, I'm alive, I'm strong and healthy
I need to be loved
My sexuality needs you
where are you?"
Dune, can you find
love as your devoted companion
in the dawn of your years
life has given to you but
a grain of sand
upon the shoreline of eternity.
Seldom has the unrestricted
reached out his hand
as you ran past the
cycles of change.
Multitudes of blank faces
stand upon the river's bank
adorned in their riches
their minds in stormy intrusion
laughing hysterically,
mocking your movements

in running to make love
for they see this as a fool's folly
as you fight their elements
in loving your way,
until the twilight of living
shrouds you in a peace
of yet another existence.
The now falling rain
washes the dust of civilization
from your strong bones
your sensual flesh
your tamed expressions, now
revealing a clean spontaneity,
a wild-like quality
as alike as the woods
that now propels you down
the corridor of your reckoning.
In their excitement
a few leaves fall from the trees
floating to an unknown.
Your heart pounds
as if yelling to be set free.
Hoards from your upbringing
swamp your mind
and are carried to the
blood of your few years.

Dune, you are a lover
a physical creature of pleasure
a mental creature of untold capacity
yet they have not set you free
but hold you in bondage
nor are they resolute in their purpose
to walk down from the bank
into the waters,
reach out and catch your body
with their ability of loving
that you may slow down
and embrace, making love
flesh to flesh,
heart to heart,
as two submerge into
the flow of the water's current
proclaiming, we are also lovers
of the same kind.



Let he who loves
step forward!

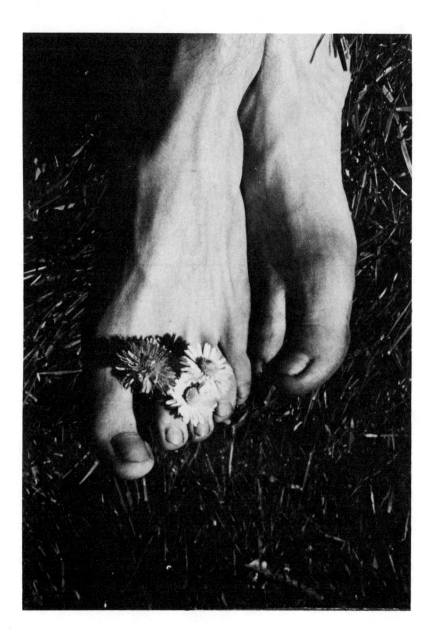

# VIII

## Observations

# When Love Looks Upon Him

Instead of walking barefoot in the sand we wear shoes for fear of stepping upon a broken shell. Does not the beauty and the sweetness of a rose grow from a thorn-filled branch?

This lad is not afraid of being naked nor does he feel the need to wear the protective clothes of pretending. He goes naked among the brambles. His body may become scratched and scarred but he is free and does not fear his feelings or new thoughts for he trusts himself to love and, if love finds him worthy, then the scratches and the scars become beautiful when love looks upon him.

# Our Environment

Our environment has a profound influence on each male in controlling his personality-behavior. Our environment can have the ability to allow the male to search for himself by freeing him from stereotyped values. When his environment imposes values for his character and those values are alien to his true nature, he finds turmoil, insecurity and anxieties within that false image the values command him to become. Since this churning continues inside him, he needs energy outlets for these frustrations. Quite often his victims are his girlfriend, his wife, his children and other males. Other males he sees living by their own values who are happier and freer in their environment are a torment to him. I have repeatedly observed these types of males strike out against males who loved other males or loved both males and females. Their vicious actions, whether verbal or physical, clearly showed their inability to cope with their own feelings because of their attachment to social values. I have also seen these same males sneak away from their normal environment to places where they could find another male for a sexual relationship. Back in their normal environment they condemn and label this action as perverted, ugly or unnatural.

A lot of males are so bound to their environmental complacency that only a catastrophe or forced change or a unique experience will alter their personality. I have on many occasions witnessed these males wrestling with value controls until time or necessity or

loving cut the umbilical cord from mother society, releasing them to personal individualism. I felt great joy in watching another male rise to a greater plateau of respect for himself and for others—another horizon for love, another spearhead for peace, another reason for eliminating wars.

# Sexual Approval

With acceptance of all types of positive interactions, sexual and sensual freedom leads to freedom in other areas of communication. Sex as an expression of oneself is an important function to a healthy body as well as a healthy mind. It releases vast amounts of energy that we quite often keep inside. This tension we repress can lead to mental breakdowns, physical sickness and a hypocritical attitude toward those who are living as others wish secretly they could. Our ability to release our sexual desires helps to focus on our individualism rather than seeing ourself as a social object. Understanding the various motives and reasons for our sexual expressions (or lack of) can help to prevent situations that otherwise might harm the beauty of the encounter or might maliciously hurt someone.

For example, a male having sexual relationships with another male in friendship I have found never makes him less of a man. On the contrary it seems to stimulate his ability to become more sensitive to other people and more aware of life around him: A male who can learn more of the nature of his body through another body like his own; a male who can become less of a warrior; a male whose loving can achieve a greater degree of compassion. Sex, with intent projected through loving, is always beautiful. Our limited experiences with the realm of body contact often confuses our sexuality and inhibits our identity.

Sex is vital and meaningful, when the motives are honorable, with any human being. Sex, unselfishly given, brings people closer together on all levels of communication, especially in the building of strong relationships.

The language of the body is as important as the language of the mind in communicating the love we feel toward each other.

125

## That Special Person

It appears to be true that too often when a person finds that "one and only love" of that special person they have little need for any other meaningful relationship. Their capacity, rather than increasing because of this special loving found, diminishes in its profound radiation to others. How tragic when we adhere to a small part of loving that special person in its total revelation. I have always felt that each time we found a special loving relationship it magnified our understanding in giving to others.

Loving other people is not enough in today's seductive society. It takes a wanting to be loved. A needing to be loved. Every particle of loving is vital and none should be turned away. We need to receive the act of loving to learn how to give love. Finding that special person, puts love into a category that will fulfill all their desires and needs and together they will live in paradise, floating upon the ocean of ecstasy, just the two of them. They will realize its fallacy when paradise is shaken by the earthquake of truth. That a special person is a vital beginning, a foundation that expands their ability to love others.

# The Common and the Ordinary

As he observed life around him he could focus on the
lesser values, the superficial reactions and the lower
level of awareness that many males held sacred in their
daily lives. He never judged that they were good or bad
under these conditions only that they caused the de-
cline of loving. He felt he must try and speak out for
the mute, the silent, the intoxicated males in his

country. He met many males drunk with mechanical thoughts. What might sober them long enough to see for the first time a more abundant life for themselves and become involved with and for the world? What stimulant might wake them from their stupor and drunkenness? "I really don't care . . . I don't want to get involved . . . I don't need to change . . . Give me the good life (money, pleasures, fun times) and the hell with everyone else . . . I don't need you . . . I've got color television and a refrigerator that makes ice cubes."

The man had also come in contact with many of the common, ordinary type of males, molded into niches by tradition. Their life of expediency to social values dominated any exchange of individual intimacy or loving that might have slipped through their shell towards him. The more intimate he became, even with simple words as a bridge, the more they would back off at a point that was unsafe or threatened their safety bubble—that impenetrable shield that protects their enlightenment from expansion. They wanted to love and be loved more than the now was realized but their indoctrination prohibited taking the chance. Even confrontation of their basic beliefs that might have been shattered in conversation or their lack of intelligent answers to questions he asked many times didn't stimulate their quest into additional knowledge. He hoped they could excel in their own discovery, finding a catalyst. Each male he met possessed a loving spirit yet was dormant in the cocoon of self-realization.

# A *Personal Statement!*

I was not born to defend my feelings.
I am here to discuss my feelings.
I was not born to be labeled or put in a tube of behavior.
I am here as a constantly growing personality.
I was not born to lead.
I am here to guide.
I was not born to command.
I am here to suggest.
I was not born to be persecuted for being different.
I am here to stimulate thinking, to be a new experience.
I was not born to be abused.
I am here to be used with kindness.

I am trying to build bridges but they are being destroyed.
Do people always want to stay on the other side?

## There Was a Man

His life has been filled
with all types of loving relationships.
Neither age, nor sex, nor race, nor religion
has prevented him from experiencing
beautiful encounters, both physical and mental,
and the building with people of their hopes
and dreams and their fantasies.

# Many Things

She sat upon the rock her fingers feeling the sensations of the moving water. This cherished place that untangled nerves, that gave nourishment to good thoughts spoke to her in the cascading of the falls as the water continued as a stream, turning into a river and finally becoming a part of the Gulf of Mexico. "Why cannot loving be as this water, becoming many things as it journeys in and out of living things?" she thought.

All kinds of loving to her were as they should be.

# A New Beginning

During the age of Western history most books about human love have followed the thoughts of male-female relationships. Sociology and psychology, the human behavior sciences, have directed the vast majority of their comments again to the male-female type of loving, giving little notice to the natural loving of one's own sex. What is mankind afraid of that it has to block out this vital form of loving directed toward meaningful human growth?

How pathetically ignorant we have let ourself become in the manifestation of our loving. We can send men to the moon and soon to other planets. We can build skyscrapers one hundred and twenty stories high. We can build computers that replace the work and minds of many people. Our scientific achievements are surpassing all else. We are developing endless comforts and pleasurable toys to play with and yet we lag so far behind in the real meaning to our existence . . . the motivation in accepting all types of love as being natural.

Isn't now the time for us to stop hiding behind a false image of masculinity, toughness, domination, obsessed with social acceptance, fear of loving other males and proceed to the sensitive, affectionate, intelligent, miracle of creation we can become.

We become what we think; only the expansion of our thinking will reveal to us—our potential as a loving person. Living has an obligation: realizing we are students of higher consciousness and needs to constantly change as does the pattern of all things. This is our responsibility. Not just to ourselves but to those we build relationships with.

I personally feel we breach universal justice when we don't or won't recognize that all kinds of loving are our greatest virtue. It seems to be learned in seeking pure knowledge and by direct experiences of the senses combined with the intellect. The purity of loving can only be gathered into our lives by an honest desire to accept all forms of love and not let others contaminate our interpretation.

I believe that man possesses a soul which existed before the body we now have and chose our body as a vehicle during a particular human life cycle. After the body dies the soul retains energy and is active in some form of intelligence and again manifests itself through another human body and another human cycle creating some form of immortality. We must search out the understanding of this soul and its relationship to our body so we don't continue to live shallow lives on the physical plane of existence. Surely we can become more balanced in our friendships with each other and more honest in our motivation.

The death of old beliefs, traditional concepts, accepted truths that we find alien to our spirit is not an end but a new beginning that launches us on a journey to fulfillment.

Someday, when we care enough to search out the truth, I think we will find that many facts and lessons of our history have been greatly misinterpreted and lost and altered to religious doctrines, dogmatic ideas and fear. *Life is so precious, how can a man live against his true nature?* How can a man face dishonor of himself when he runs away from any form of love? We must find the courage to live what we believe is good and make a stand against any law or moral that we find unjust.

Personally I feel as long as I breathe life and have the freedom of my faculties I shall pursue a philosophical course and speak and write and share with any person, what I have discovered to be the truth. Every person I chance to meet I will try and persuade them to perfect their state of loving and stimulate their exploration of change, Without consciously manipulating or forcing that change.

The myth of the Phoenix, a symbol of one life ending and the same life beginning anew, may be a universal truth that has eluded mankind. The Phoenix, a bird which burned itself in a fire after living for hundreds of years, then rose from the ashes in the radiant flower of youth to live through yet another cycle of years. Growing old mentally, the body's rapid aging, the restrictions we place on ourselves, seem to be a one-way path on a straight line leading to decay and loneliness. The myth of the Phoenix may hold more truth than man vaguely realizes.

We've got to get ready to help each other launch mankind into a new era of understanding. This can be our renaissance for the twentieth century.

Each of us, in our own way, should start reaching out with encouragement and acceptance, and use more of our resources in showing love to both males and females. We must probe deeply into life and bring to the surface what we discover there. We have this obligation not only to each other but to the children we bring into this world. They must be our reason, for the child in us and the children are innocent. Maybe someday there can be a world without partitions of the heart.

It takes courage to love.